JUST A WOMAN
Poetry, Prose & Homespun Recipes

by
Lauvonda Lynn (Meade) Young

Happy reading,

Lynn Young

Cedar Creek Publishing
Virginia, USA

Feb 2012

30537 7903
A

Cover photo by Larry Rubendall

Cedar Creek Publishing
Bremo Bluff, Virginia
www.cedarcreekauthors.com

Printed in the United States of America

Library of Congress Control Number 2011923881

ISBN 978-0-9659419-5-2

DEDICATION

This publication is dedicated to
the special men in my life:

Robert Paul Meade—my father, the one from whom I learned life's important lessons; I always thought he was proud of my poetry;

Carl Edward Young, Jr.—my deceased spouse of thirty-four years; my first mentor in the art of giving and receiving love; he strongly supported my writing;

Robert Preston Meade—my brother, the man who has shown me by example that we must keep our hearts smiling in the face of adversary;

Litz Andrew Young—my empathetic son and friend, the one who taught me to love unconditionally and profoundly; and

Larry Lee Rubendall—my husband and dearest life partner, the one who was not afraid to pick up the pieces of my broken heart and give me the promise of tomorrow; he has been a tremendous supporter of my work.

Advance Reviews for
Just a Woman

"This is a book of memories. In this group of poems framed by commentary and reminiscences, the writer records a lifetime's joys, sorrows, aspirations, and achievements. Throughout it is enlivened and made poignant by the writer's eye for the telling detail: kisses occur in a dilapidated smokehouse; a bouquet of flowers is $3.99 at Food Lion. If this awareness of the circumstances in which we pursue our dreams can sometimes make the writer feel 'shackled by reality,' it also embodies her heartening conviction that 'this day is yours.'"
Kenny Marotta

"Lauvonda Lynn (Meade) Young's book of poems and commentaries creates a unique portrait of a life lived in the fullness of love and wonder, pain and loss. Young is both loyal to her past, treasuring the memories of people and places, and eager to embrace a 'fresh start' in a new home where 'my unfettered heart / will breathe anew.' She is a vivid storyteller, guiding us through her hometown of Tazewell, Virginia, her father's farm, and her grandma's 'time-worn' house, through the joys of parenting and creating and the horror of sudden loss. In her charming disclaimer, 'Far Short of a Classic,' she compares herself to 'a worn-out book' – *No time to rearrange the words / upon virginal pages / No time to create the great classic / I yearned incessantly to be.* Young's modesty, though admirable, should not obscure the fact that she is a compassionate observer, who has written a generous, life-affirming book."

Sharon Leiter

"Lauvonda Lynn (Meade) Young writes in the tradition of American female pioneer poets who travel into their own memories and experiences to mine the mysteries and strengths of the human heart. A rabbi once commented that the face of God looks like the faces of all the people who have loved us. Young's work is full of those faces: her parents and grandparents, siblings, her son, her first husband, Eddie, who died suddenly, and her husband Larry. In her work, Young does not avert her gaze from life's tragedies; rather she looks steadily into those experiences and greets them, not just with grief appropriate, but also with the strength and positive attitude of her foremothers, like her Grandmother Fletcher. Lauvonda Lynn (Meade) Young has traveled far from her roots in southwest Virginia, but her poetry illustrates that the meaning of home resides ultimately in the human heart."

Jewell-Ann Parton

TABLE OF CONTENTS

INTRODUCTION

The quote below clearly denotes why writing poetry is such an essential part of my life. The truth is that writing poetry completes my life. It is my hobby, therapy, escape, favorite past-time, and my passion. Writing poetry is the greatest gift I have given to myself.

Just A Woman has been birthed for several reasons. First and foremost, while I never set a goal or had an expectation of being published, I always had a dream. It is marvelous that my dream will be realized. The most satisfying reason, yet to be realized, is that it will be extremely gratifying if I am told that reading *Just a Woman* was an enjoyable experience.

Lauvonda Lynn (Meade) Young

*I write poetry solely because
it is manna for my soul.*

SPECIAL THANKS

I acknowledge and thank my friend, **Reverend Dr. Jewell-Ann Parton**, an extraordinary professor of English literature, published writer, and creative writing teacher, for all I learned under her tutelage when I was a student at Piedmont Virginia Community College in Charlottesville, Virginia. I owe Jewell-Ann a great deal of gratitude for early on helping me to believe my writing had merit, and more recently I am indebted to her for performing the ceremony (June 9, 2007) when I married Larry Lee Rubendall.

I also am deeply grateful to **Kenny Marotta,** the humble man who asked that no titles be attached to his name, the one who allowed me to impose on his time and busy schedule to look over my poetry manuscript. Marotta, an outstanding teacher, mentor, and gentle critic of my work, is another person who has had a huge significance in my writing life.

Deep appreciation also is extended to **Sharon Leiter**, my friend and former neighbor, who also let me impinge upon her time to review my manuscript. Leiter has made marvelous contributions to the literary world, and to educating others, and she and I share a love of all things Emily Dickinson. Leiter has published two books of poetry: *The Lady and the Bailiff of Time* and *The Dream of Leaving*.

My spouse, **Larry Rubendall**, has my heartfelt thanks for supplying the black and white photograph used on the front cover of my book of poetry; he took this photo when we vacationed in 2007 in Lake George, New York.

Thanks also are extended to "TP" (whose name I can't remember or decipher on the drawing) of Stuart Pharmaceutical, who did the caricature of me on Page 10 in this book. (I briefly crossed paths with TP at the annual meeting of the American College of Physicians, San Francisco, California, in 1987).

The final person that is due special thanks is **Linda Layne**, Publisher/Consultant, Cedar Creek Publishing. Linda is greatly rewarding me by publishing my first book of poetry. I will be eternally grateful to her.

MY FIRST POEM

My first poem, "Spring Plowing," was likely penned in 1962 when I was a junior in high school. It was accepted for publication in 1963, in *Young America Sings, National High School Poetry Anthology.*

There is a history to the writing of "Spring Plowing." It was written after my English teacher rejected the prose piece I had submitted as my major writing project for the semester. My work was returned to me with written instruction to redo the ending because my ending "sounded too similar to Margaret Mitchell's *Gone With The Wind.*"

I initially was insulted that my teacher essentially accused me of plagiarizing, because at the time I had not yet read Mitchell's book or seen any film version of it. Today I am honored to have been associated, even in a miniscule way, with such a well-known writer.

I didn't think I could complete a new ending to my story before the specified deadline, and I certainly did not have time to develop a new piece of prose, so I decided to compose a poem.

The inspiration for this poem was my father's farm. My father was a coal miner, so I don't know how he mined and farmed. We had about 15 acres, a vegetable garden, a cow or two, several pigs, and sometimes a few chickens. I am sure Dad farmed mostly to put food on the table, but I like to think farming was his escape from job and life stresses, the same escape I experience when I write.

In spite of all the hubbub that preceded the writing of "Spring Plowing," I suppose my teacher was impressed with my new submission because she entered the poem in a contest. I am still in awe my first poem was published.

SPRING PLOWING

My heart leaps forward as winter
vanishes and spring appears once more
for then it's time to plow again
in the fields that slept before.

I love to take my plow at dawn
as I simply turn every furrow
my heart sings a happy song
and I eagerly await each tomorrow.

I crush the dirt within my palm
and sniff the cool, fresh soil
it makes me feel close to my land
as I welcome the day's long toil.

I linger a while after work is done
and the sun is fading away
to give some thanks, alone—
to let the good Earth have her say.

For many this land is nothing
but it means the world to me
with the help of God and nature
I find strength to plant the seed.

HOME

I once read a statement that implied we are shaped by our dwellings. I believe the "dwelling" referenced not only means the physical structures we live in, but also the places where we were born, those places where we lived as children and young adults. I think as we age home becomes the images we have stored in the attics of our minds— images revisited through memory, or through our writing or orally telling stories of our lives. We keep making mental visits, keep retelling our stories, so that our childhoods won't dissipate like fine dust in a gusty wind.

Much also has been said about not being able to reside in the place of our birth after we mature and have experienced life in another place, usually after we have exited a small town and lived for years in a large city, or what equates to a large city in comparison to the place we left. For a variety of reasons, I probably am one of those people who would no longer acclimate well to living in the town where I was born, Tazewell, Virginia, a small mining town located in the southwestern part of the state. Even though I never will physically reside in Tazewell again, I do often return in memory, and my memories grow sweeter and more precious as the years pass.

While I have not forgotten the unpleasant experiences that occurred when I was young, nowadays I tend to soften the hard edges of the reminiscences. I realize that my life was enormously enriched and shaped by the experiences of growing up in Tazewell. I am very proud of my birthplace, and ruminating about life in my coal-mining community now is a pleasant pastime.

Home means so many different things at varying times to each of us. For me, it's play time with brothers and sisters—playing tag; soft ball; pretend grown-up things (dressing up; putting on make-up; and being "mommy"); hopscotch; pretend school; board games; playing cards; hide-and-seek; and catching Fire Flies in a jar. It was a time of living and learning together. It was time spend with a childhood friend who remains a "best bud" throughout life—mine since grade school is July (Silcox) Presley.

The biggest life lesson I have learned is that home is the family, not the dwelling. Thinking about the "old days" conjures up wonderful memories of gathering family and friends around a table laden with food, where mothers sat with their babies in their laps (or I was allowed to feed or entertain the baby while the mother otherwise was occupied; I loved taking care of the babies).

Food and fellowship was the way country folk entertained. Everyone had large gardens, nut and fruit trees, and berry picking produced delectable jams and jellies, and fruit pies. Most mothers canned. Freezers always were stocked with beef, pork and chickens, and occasionally some deer or rabbit meat. My Uncle Delbert Fletcher prepared a wonderful squirrel dish—the only time I've eaten squirrel, and while there were few fishermen in our family, Uncle Delbert often had fresh fish that he caught and prepared (and he still does).

I have the most wonderful memories of visiting my grandmothers, American (Powers) Fletcher and Mary (Moore) Meade, especially the Sunday visits, a tradition which afforded time to visit with many family members often not seen otherwise. Grandma Fletcher did not prepare "fancy food," but there always was plenty to eat at her house, and she generally had homemade pickles, jelly, and other delights such as picked corn. Grandma Meade was well known for her huge biscuits, chocolate syrup, and churned butter that she fed her children and grandchildren for breakfast; we all loved this meal, served with our very own bottle of RC Cola. My mother, Wanda Lee (Fletcher) Meade, wasn't a "fancy cook" either, but my taste buds get stimulated just thinking about her Hamburger Spaghetti (all ingredients cooked together in a pot on the electric stove); and her Meatloaf (made in an electric skillet); Fried Green Tomatoes; and Applesauce Cake. Eating at my mother-in-law's house—Eleanor (Gildersleeve) Young, was a gastronomical delight. Her cooking expertise was widely known and admired, especially her skill at making yeast breads and rolls. Mom Eleanor did more than put food on the table. Her table always was overflowing with at least one dish that a member of her family favored, an endeavor that made all of us feel special. Several of Eleanor's recipes can be found in the back of this book. From these women, I learned the value of communing with loved ones around the table. Such meals not only nurtured bodies, but also minds as we engaged in lively conversation, including debating the events of the day.

The most important lesson I have learned from my life experiences, is that it really does not matter where we live if we live happily in the place we call home.

SOUTHWEST VIRGINIA THREADS OF LIFE

I sometimes dig up majestic effigies, catalogued in the vaults of my mind, to visit places, tightly trussed to my childhood memories. There were towns or communities, called Jewell Ridge and Bishop, where men made their living, digging black chunks of coal, out of the ground.

Miners lived in identical white-washed or shingled houses, littered on hills, like polka dots. One thriving mining wick was Amonate, for a time home to my father, while he morphed into manhood. Coal and the railroad, helped Pocahontas develop a significant presence in the area.

My father's parents, the Meades, lived on Dry Fork. Grandpa, known as Papa to all, built my Aunt Marty a superb, miniature version of his homeplace: a tiny house complete with attic storage and a front porch, where Marty and I, dolls in tow, spent hours using her "Easy Bake Oven," while completing pretend, grown-up, domestic chores.

Riverjack was the place where my Mother's parents, the Fletchers, lived. Grandma Fletcher, stitched densely into my essence, still influences my life daily.

Riverjack, connected by Hubble Hill to Baptist Valley, was the community where my childhood exited and adolescence flourished. This reminiscing threads my past to the present: each stitch sewn with infinite love.

MY HOMETOWN

I flamed through my teenage years in Tazewell:
    a small town, rooted in a far corner, of
    southwest Virginia, a place once filled
    with Norman Rockwell beauty.

Jimmy's, the area's lone food joint,
    located at Four Way, was where
    the in-crowd gathered. Waitresses
    in tight skirts and form-fitting sweaters,
    delivered hamburgers and French fries, to
    customers in cars: patrons who would not talk:
    too busy, seat dancing, snapping fingers, as
    Elvis' velvet voice, spilled out the radio.

We gathered in Jimmy's back parlor;
    guys played Pin Ball for nickel bets;
    girls sipped Cherry Cokes; nibbled
    barbeque potato chips; patiently waited,
    to catch the eye of one fellow or another.

Couples hooked up toward evening's end;
    headed to Goose Creek, to complete a
    hurried up whatever; hormones got sated;
    girls missed 10:00 p.m. curfews; angry dads,
    always were waiting at the front door.

Continued

Life worsened for some as months moved
    along; periods didn't come; reality hit; dreams
    evaporated; girls realized, babies growing
    in their youthful bellies soon would be
    sucking pacifier's; riding their ballooning hips.

Parents' worn-out jalopies, carried us to
    the drive-in theater Saturday nights; bodies
    were laid out on back seats, so we could
    feel each other up. Glimpses of John Wayne,
    chasing bad guys across the screen, we
    caught, because inquisitions had to be
    answered every Sunday.

A less favorite place to congregate, was the
    bowling alley, postured on the northern
    end of town, near the A-Mart; geezers
    boozed; leered at girls in gossamer
    dresses; balls rolled anyway; empty
    pockets couldn't imagine a trip to
    Bluefield, to seek other amusements.

There were professionals of necessity:
    a few lawyers, a doctor or two, a dentist:
    But coal miners were the giants, who
    made mountains move, as they dug
    black diamonds out of pits in the ground:

Continued

Sometimes coal couldn't be shoveled,
so miners talked, about life in and
around the hole: picket lines, fights,
gun shots, explosions.

Things have changed in Tazewell. The mines
shut down. Welfare lines bulge. Aged miners need
blocked cheese. A neon-lighted, multiplex replaced
the drive-in theater. Jimmy's restaurant was
demolished. A used car lot sprawls brashly on that
acreage. No one knows what happened to Jimmy.

I have a great fondness for this poem because it provides a plethora of imagery of small-town life.

FRESH START

I'm looking for a new house,
so I can escape:
aged ghosts hovering,
disappointments proliferating,
memories metastasized,
decaying life, ballooning in veins.

In my new home,
my unfettered heart,
will breathe anew:
budding dreams,
unpacked,
will be sprinkled
in virginal corners
to await maturation:
Tomorrow's promises
harvested,
will be devoured,
enthusiastically.

IF ONLY

I pummel the twisted pot-holed highway
out of Gratton, on my way into town.
Lawyers and real estate agents, will be
annoyed. I'm late—they wait, to close
sale on my parents' home. I apply
pressure to the gas pedal. The car lunges
forward with renewed energy. Pot-holes
and speeding do not mesh, with my need
to drink in Tazewell's beauty, unequaled
anywhere:

> emerald hills,
> crystal clear creeks.
> chaste, cotton-candy clouds,
> hugging the boulders,
> at the top of the Peak,
> the place where Indian drawings,
> by a tribe unknown, can be found.

Each time I'm transported, to this place
of my birth, in this treasured corner, of
southwest Virginia, nature nips at my
battered soul, beckoning me to migrate
home to the locale, where living is much
less paradoxical. Residing again in
Tazewell, would be impossible for me,
of course, because I am enslaved to city
life, and all its trappings.

TRUTH

It's not true that we can't
go home again.

Trips just can't be made
by boat, on a train,
in automobiles, or on foot.

A memory past begins a journey,
in our truth-seeking, rational brain.

Reminiscences move along:
down pulsating highways,
into our loving,
benevolent hearts—the place
where our hurts are healed
and we find shelter for our souls.

PUBLISHED

My published poems, or contest winners, have been written over the course of my life, beginning with the first poem I wrote in 1962. Prior to 1962, I wrote short stories or vignettes. When I was a working wife and mother, and also a college student, I went years without writing anything creatively. I have renewed my passion for writing poetry, and I hope to keep my pen moving furiously in future years.

SANCTUARY

Grandma's house is time-worn,
paint is peeling, hinges are rusty,
but I still love to visit there;

Peace abounds between the walls,
amongst old lace and antiques,
security is fostered in familiarity;

Under ancient, moss-covered eaves,
hope sprouts like spring flowers:
Grandma nurtures tender dreams.

Published–American Anthology of Southern Poetry; Dreams and Other Bargains; and The Piedmont Writer, Vol. II.
This poem was written in honor of my beloved maternal Grandmother, American Lee (Powers) Fletcher. She was known as "Maw" by her grandchildren.

REGENERATION

Give me not a winter death,
of floed rivers
and denuded trees . . .

come for me in the spring
when scarlet tulips kindle
the emerald loam . . .

then, with thoughts of my
rebirth looming, I will
obligingly accept departure . . .

Published–The Piedmont Writer
This poem was written for my deceased sister-in-law, Ramona Kay (Brown) Meade, who died in her early thirties from complications of a malignant brain tumor.

LOVE SONG

Your body sings
next
to
mine:
in perfect harmony, we
cantillate our melody:
well-tuned instruments
taut
and
vibrant:
we forge a Cantata.

Published–Branches in My Hand

PLEASURE

My old book of poems:
read so many times,
its binding has come unglued.

I wonder if I can read it,
one time more, before I'm
forced to throw it away.

Published–The Piedmont Writer
    Collecting books of poetry is one of my passions, and I never can recycle one. In fact, I can't part with any book I purchase or receive as a gift. Books call to me when I enter a bookstore, or an antique shop; I obtain books at flea markets, yard and estate sales. Library sales are heavenly. I also have been known to snatch one or two books out of a recycle bin. Cookbook collecting is a favorite pastime. I buy cookbooks, old and used, when I travel, and most any other time (my collection likely numbers over 300, including paperbacks). My book collecting has probably developed into an obsession, but it is one that I will gladly endure, for the pleasure of being surrounded by words (and recipes).

BIRTH OF A POET

A
writer
becomes
a poet
when
words
and
images
force
an
emotion.

Published–The Piedmont Writer

THE POWER OF POWER

Women
have{no]
poHER
man
he got
it
all "!"

        or
        duz
        men
        jUS)t
        th(I)nk
        so

                (WE)FE-
                males
                have
                po(HER)
                too—
                tho
                (W
                        E)
                don't
                need
                none
                /2/
                m.a.k.e.
                (US)
                whole
                        •

"The Power of Power" was published in The College Paper (Piedmont Virginia Community College, Volume II, No. 6, April 16, 1990). It was part of an article I wrote entitled "Some Thoughts on Power."

The writing of "The Power of Power" was inspired by the work of E. E. Cummings whose poetry I find fascinating because of the way he splatters some poems upon the page and because of his unusual use of punctuation.

*This next poem also plays on the writing style of E.E. Cummings. It was published in **Branches in My Hand.***

EE CUMM UP ANCE

!Big boss
  Dick
    Tator,

Ball
Break
HER

(he who has none of his own)

DEMANDING
        (WHY?)
t
  o
    m
      a
        k
          e

him
Self
           Felt
      Like

POISON
SUMAC

                On
               A
                  Hot
                    Summer
                      Night.

MY SWEET BABY

Carried you for nine months
protected in a pouch

never knew how wonderful
life would be when you got out

tiny, fragile
baby extraordinaire
smelling all sweet and new

wrinkled little bundle
how dearly I love you.

Published–The Piedmont Writer
   *Nature unfortunately denied me a pregnancy, but my
poem, "My Sweet Baby," is how I would have felt had I carried
and birthed a child. While denied the experience of a pregnancy,
I did become a mother. One of the greatest joys of my life has been
mothering my adopted son, Litz Andrew Young. I often think of
the quote, author unknown, that he "Did not grow under my
heart, but in it." Mothering is not about pregnancy; it is about
love.*

PLACE UPON MY GRAVE STONE –
SHE WAS MY WIFE: I LOVED HER

I tried to be a rose
fragrant and beautiful
but my thorns were all you saw:

I wanted to be a prism
colorful and many-faceted
but you shut out my sunbeam:

I struggled to be a bird
unrestrained and free
but you clipped my wings.

Published–Branches in my Hand
    "Place Upon My Grave Stone: She Was My Wife: I Loved Her" was written long before the title was selected. The poem initially was not intended to be about a couple, but the poem just wasn't working with any of the numerous titles I identified until the current title evolved.

THERAPY

I love lying
at ocean's edge . . .

Snuggled in a
bed of cool sand . . .

Surf nipping
dreamingly
on my toes . . .

Sunbeams
promenading
fun-lovingly . . .

Published–The Piedmont Writer

FLOWERS

I arrange the fresh
cut flowers in a vase . . .
a $3.99 special
from the Food Lion . . .
These flowers, are just as
beautiful, on our dining room
table, as any I've ever seen . . .
although *My Love,*
they aren't from you.
A tear slides, down my cheek,
when I remember, how much
you adored showering me, with
flowers. You ran, all over town,
to search out, a "Friday Special" . . .
If the special didn't suit, or supplies
were depleted, you bought flowers
anyway, probably deciding the thing
you would do without, the following
week, because we had no extra money,
to purchase flowers . . . It didn't matter,
you gave flowers to impress, *Your Love* . . .
I heard you, with my heart . . .

Published–A Shimmer On The Horizon
    The "you" in this poem is my deceased husband, Carl
Edward Young, Jr., whom I married at age 18. We were married
thirty-four years before he died unexpectedly in 1996.

AN ETERNITY IN THE QUIET ROOM
(Waiting For Death)

I'm ushered into the Quiet Room.

I think Nurse B doesn't want me
present, when the Rescue Squad,
brings you into the
Emergency Department;
but I want, need to, stand
by your side.

What happened?
Was there a car accident?
Maybe you were hit,
While working on a bridge,
something, you always feared.

No one brings me information.
What if's and *why's* spin in my brain.
Isolation in this square box is smothering.
I'm good for nothing. Can't even pray.

I suppose you're alive.
I don't know.
You must be alive.
They would tell me.

Continued

You can't be dead.
You are too healthy.

Doctors will fix the wrong.
I believe . . . in the physicians.

Rescue Squad squeals in.
Hall noise seeps under the door.
I attach images to sounds: likely
the transport cart you lie upon,
just crashed into a wall; rescue
personnel—nurses—have
collided in their quest to do
their jobs; fluid bottles swing
unruly: organized chaos, it
sometimes is called, all part of
the urgent care process. But
loved one's gets fixed; they
go home. Will I take you home?

Lots of voices.
Not your voice.
No talking. Not good.
You're unconscious? Dead?

Noise moves on.
I wish I could go to you.
Can't. They need to do their work.
I should stay out of the way.

Continued

I'll wait some more.

Dr. C joins me.
Sits on a stool.
I see him peripherally.
His muteness is comforting.
Language isn't necessary.
What is there to say anyway?

I twirl my wedding band; it
constantly circles my finger.
The repetition forces my brain
to focus; disjointed thoughts
are temporarily calmed.

I don't make any noise.
This is the Quiet Room.
Thundering hearts must
be subdued.

Wait some more.

How long has it been?
A half hour? An hour?
More?

It's hot.

Silence—except for my
heart, hammering in my ears.

Continued

I'm growing impatient;
begin fidgeting; brush loose
hair from my dress; pick
at nothing in the pattern.

I guess you still are alive.
Are you? It's been a long time.
Too long for your brain to be
deprived of oxygen.

More waiting: When will
I know something?

I wish I could pray for you,
But words heavy as stones
lay incapacitated on my tongue.

My faith is paper thin,
but I'm trusting the doctors
will save you.

My head aches.
I need water.

Dr. P comes in.
Asks for names of family to call.
Wants to know if I have a minister.

Continued

"No minister," I say, "Just my son—
our son. His name is Andrew."
My response is scribbled on her pad.

Our eyes make contact.
I feel death.
A scream balloons in my heart.

She tells me they can't sustain a heart beat.
Some sparks. That's all. They think you
suffered a heart attack.

A heart attack?
Oh God. Oh God.
You're too young. Only 56.
You never are ill.

I try not to know,
but, I know.
You're dying.
You may be dead.

I can't breathe.
Anger flames.

God can't have you.

Continued

Doctors can't save you.
God won't help.
He wants to punish me,
for backsliding.
He is going to let you die.

It's my fault.
I'm so sorry.

Nurse Kim, my friend,
appears, asks if she can
contact Andrew. I supply
his place of employment.
Don't know the phone number.

Andy arrives. Sits beside me
on the sofa. Asks what
happened. Gives me a hug
when I tell him you may
be dying.

We wait for what is to be.
Listen to minutes creep.
Accept the stillness.

Dr. L. comes to confirm your death.
He says it as kindly as he can.
His words suck up all the oxygen.

Continued

Nurse C appears; asks if I want
to see you. "Yes" is enough.

I go to you. Touch your face.
Kiss your lips. Try to breathe
Life into you. It's impossible.
Nothing lives—except perhaps
the strands of your hair that I
twist around my finger.

Your body already is cooling.

How can I bear this?

I must stay strong for Andy,
standing at my side, looking broken.
Will I have the strength, to glue our
lives back together?

Published–A Poem For Your Thoughts
   *This poem is about my experience in the Emergency
Department (Department of Emergency Medicine, University of
Virginia Medical Center, Charlottesville, Virginia) the day my
first husband, Carl Edward Young, Jr., died. Eddie, as he most
often was called, was born December 23, 1942. He died on his
birthday, December 23, 1996, which to-date I recognize as the
most horrible day of my life.*

VISIT AT DAD'S GRAVE

A whorled oak,
flings a spidery shadow,
across iridescent squares of green,
edged orderly side by side,
in this hapless place,
where old bones lie eternally.

Summer gulps its last breaths,
leaves unhurriedly prepare for
their fall cavalcade, while all of nature,
begins promenading, into another season.

If only my faith was as strong as yours,
I could believe that, just as the seasons
resurrect perpetually, you metamorphosed,
out of your moldy coat, put on a
new body and face, dressed again in spring
raiments, traveled to Heaven on ethereal
wings. If only I could believe, I would no
longer, be shackled to reality.

Published–The Blue Ridge Anthology 2007
The "you" in this poem is my father, Robert Paul Meade.
He died in May 2002, at age 73. I needed more time with him!

Punctuated
Underlined
Boxed-in
    Parenthesis
Folded
Stitched
Hemmed
    Embroidered
Mashed
Dashed
Slashed
    Diced
Finished
Period
The-End
    WOMAN

Published–Branches in My Hand

*   "Woman" was composed the semester I took a college class
(Piedmont Virginia Community College, Charlottesville, Virginia)
entitled "Women in Literature," a course where most of the prose
and poetry was about oppressed women or oppressive life situations.*

FAR SHORT OF A CLASSIC

I AM
a worn-out book
tattered and yellowed
musty and mildewed
stunned by my uselessness:

perfectly syntactical
grammatically correct
but capped and compromised
in meaningless sentences:

unworthy of the 25-cent sale
discarded into the trash bin
to suffocate under dirty rags
and odious cigarette butts:

No time to rearrange the words
upon virginal pages.
No time to create the great classic
I yearned incessantly to be.

Published—Branches in My Hand
I find it interesting that "Far Short of A Classic" and "Just" ended up side by side in my poetry book, since one poem starts with the words "I AM" and the other ends with the words "I AM." This happenstance was not planned; the two poems actually were written years apart.

JUST

I ain't no Grace Kelly
Articulate, perfect, princess
I am Cinderella's mother-in-law.

I ain't no Jackie Kennedy
Affluent, rich American
I am Loretta, a coal miner's daughter.

I ain't no Elizabeth Barrett Browning
Writer extraordinaire
I am just a woman—but I AM.

Published–Dreams and Other Bargains

"Just" reveals a great deal about me—most notably that I am the daughter of a coal miner. When I was very young, and stupid, I wasn't so proud of my father's occupation. I guess I foolishly thought my dad should be a doctor, or a minister, or a postmaster (those city jobs). When I matured and gained some wisdom (I hope), I realized my father had a difficult and dangerous job that he loved and excelled at doing. He made good money, and our family most always had more than the necessities. I learned the positive impact mining had on the economy in our town and surrounding areas, and I started appreciating and eventually caring about my father's occupation.

I actually wanted to entitle my first book of poetry, Another Coal Miner's Daughter, but feared copyright infringement problems if I used any version of Loretta Lynn's book, Coal Miner's Daughter. I, therefore, chose the next best title, the words Just A Woman.

CONTEST WINNERS

In 2003, the Joint Conference of the American Society on Aging (National Council on Aging) sponsored their first contest of poetry and photography entitled, "Crossing the Great Divide." Three poems could be submitted. I placed first in poetry for these first three poems.

SEARCHING

God: I never thought
You to be vengeful.
I don't believe You wrenched
away the love of my life,
just to punish, although . . .

God: such gleaning, fails to render
solace for my anguished soul . . .

God: You gave no insight,
to help me cling to fragile beliefs . . .

God: Prove to me, You are real.
Come: Place healing balm,
upon my blistered heart . . .

IN A DARK PLACE

I wanted to hold on to my grief
. . . bind it tautly to me
. . . wallow unabashedly in pain
. . . continue the flood of salty tears
. . . persist in picking at my raw heart
I felt as dead as You. Wished I was:
. . . until You came to me in a dream
. . . forced me out of the abyss
. . . told me to get on with living:

I did.

ENDINGS AND BEGINNINGS

I go into another man's arms
without guilt, because
I dealt with this emotion
in my dreams . . .

All those dreams that invaded my
sleep after your death, when you
came to me after I was sexually
sated, from an encounter
with a faceless stranger.

I would awaken in tears of distress
After saying, *I thought you were dead.*

You never gave me a reply in my dreams—
I think because I needed to supply the
response myself.

And I have.
You would tell me:
This day is yours.
Make the most of it.
Be happy.

. . . and so, I can lie blissfully,
in the arms of another
knowing I have your approval.

I still occasionally have dreams about my deceased spouse "returning from the dead." In my dream, I attempt to continue life as it was before he died, but I have difficulty because my life has changed so drastically. It would be nice to know the message this dream holds for me; maybe I have "survivor's guilt." Maybe it is just a recurring dream.

MEMORIES

I prepared today the first,
Fried Green tomatoes,
I've had since your death.

I devoured them eagerly,
as I remembered fondly how
you lovingly cooked them for me.

I would gorge myself,
eating leftovers for breakfast,
(all doused with ketchup, of course).

Little things we experienced
together, have forged such vivid,
sweet memories in my mind's eye.

Memories are all I have left:
recollections that remind me,
how deeply you were stitched,
into the fabric of my life.

Editor's Choice Award–Poetry Guild, 1998.
Published–A Shimmer On the Horizon, Poetry Guild (1998)
The "you" in this poem is my deceased spouse, Carl Edward Young, Jr. (known as Eddie).

SISTERS ON A FETTERED PATH

It isn't necessary for me

to chisel life's muteness
upon ashen pages

to stitch boiling discontent
into endurance

or be a marble Virgin
to evade Purgatory . . . because

Emily haunted before me.

*First Place–Poetry and Best Work Overall–Writers Club,
Poetry & Prose Contest (1989), Piedmont Virginia Community
College (Charlottesville, Virginia).
Published–Branches in My Hand, and The Piedmont Writer
    (I won $25.00 in the poetry contest, and $100 for Best Work
Overall—the first monetary awards I ever received for a contest
entry. I was pumped!)
    The "Emily" in this poem is Emily Dickinson, my favorite
female poet.*

GARDENING

I tore into a poem the other day
plucked out all the weeds that were
strangling the new-fledged words
I have been nurturing so patiently.
Carelessly placed adjectives and
unnecessary commas were obliterated.
All flowery phrases swiftly disappeared.
I used my new red-handled spade to
vigorously cull unwanted clichés.
Numerous plants were deadheaded.
Seeds were gathered and scattered to
germinate anew in another poem.
Several innovative nouns were
meticulously chosen to add zest.
Thorns, rot, and decayed roots, all
were expertly excised and discarded.
I'll plant my new stanzas in neat rows,
trim new growth to perfection, pick
bloomed poems at just the right moment.

Second Place–Poetry, 2008 Blue Ridge Chapter,
Virginia Writers Club Writing Contest.
Published–The Blue Ridge Anthology 2009
    (For the second time, I won a monetary award for a poem
that placed in a contest. My bank account is growing!)

LOVE, LOSS & ENDURANCE

The greatest tragedy of loving is the loss that occurs through life changes such as the break-up of a friendship, divorce, or the most devastating of all, death. However, life would be meaningless without love.

Just as there are numerous forms and degrees of love, there also are many forms of death. This section includes some poems about other forms of death we experience. These poems include "Prose Poem for Mother (1)," which highlights the impact of dementia and a decaying body in general, and "Wishing," which speaks of the loss a mother feels after her son matures and leaves home.

MARKING HIS TERRITORY

Crayon marks on the walls
carpets stained by muddy tiny boy shoes
teething marks on the stereo cabinet
baby finger smudges everywhere.
My infant son has been busy imprinting.

"Marking His Territory" is about beginning and ending. New life can be seen in the child and his activities. The end to come (not spelled out in the poem) is the maturation of the child, his eventual leaving the home and his mother to undertake new ventures. While adulthood and separation from parents is a normal life cycle, a mother's heart never willingly lets go.

NEW PARTNER NAMED GRIEF

My sunshine disappeared into the abyss
where your putrid soul resides, that
crisp December morn in 1996, when you
arrived to tell me my spouse was dead.

You offered me a bilious cup of tea,
companioned with frigid stone rolls,
alleged more of the same could be
expected, since you were going to be
my ever present companion.

You gleefully told me straight away
your greatest joy was constant jabbing
at an abscessed spirit, too broken to fight
back. As new owner of my tranquility,
you let it be known I could forget about
putting down my frazzled nerves, for
even a minute of treasured rest.

I cringed when you told me attempts to
eject you from my existence would be
an asinine endeavor, since it was your
intent to ride my back into infinity.

*This is a poem in memory of my deceased spouse, Carl Edward
Young, Jr.*

WISHING
(A Poem For My Son, Litz Andrew Young)

I hunger for times of long ago
to hear my child beg, with
anticipation clinging, to his
words, *May I go play in the snow?*
Frozen pants, wet floors, and head colds
I gladly would endure, if only I could hear,
May I stay out a little longer? Please.

It would just be music to my ears,
if he could cry out again at three a.m.,
More orange juice. Juice. Juice.
How comforting it would be, to feel
him crawl into our bed once more, and
say, *Let me sleep in here tonight.*
I sure would love to have the chance. to
tell him it was okay to suck his thumb.
Instead of, *Son, please take your thumb
out of your mouth.* How sweet it would be,
to have him tell me I skipped a section of
the book I was reading . . . because he had
memorized the parts that he liked best.

There are no wee footprints in the snow,
no brown-eyed babe seeking my comfort,
because my child now is an adult.
Death cruelly took his father at an early age.
I sit alone, lights extinguished,
deeply enveloped in thoughts about what
I should, or could, have done, yesterday.

IF
(A Poem for My Father: Robert Paul Meade)

I sit on your grave. Distressed.
Rigid as the denuded oak tree
up on the hill—the one waiting
patiently for spring and rebirth.

If God is in Heaven,
He has released your soul from the bronze
box I placed you in that day in May, when
the clouds wept shamelessly.

If God is in Heaven,
you now are residing in a mansion,
walking on streets of gold, because
this is what He promised, and you
believed Him.

If God is in Heaven,
He would not have cheated us,
out of our goodbyes, while
physicians sliced and diced,
ripped out a cancerous kidney,
scraped the metastasis from your spine—
all the while working feverishly, to save
a decaying body, instead of helping me,
and others prepare for your death.

Continued

If God is in Heaven,
He would have given us a little more time,
so that I could have told you how proud
I was of my coal-mining father,
and you could have told me, all those
things I wanted to know about you,
including how it felt to be dying—
not physically but emotionally.

If God is in Heaven,
He would give me back my father.

The day my father learned he had a cancerous kidney, he said, "Well, I guess it is time to get my house in order." From that day forward, he began preparing for death, often telling me each day as I left him at the hospital, "I'm praying God will take me during the night." He never questioned his plight. I think he was extremely brave.

FIGHTING FOR SURVIVAL

This is the second beach vacation
without you . . . *My Spouse* . . .
You who died without warning
on a hostile winter day in 1996.

The sun still finds it pleasurable,
to warm my motionless body, as
I sit ensconced, where the ocean
gently kisses the consenting sand.
I watch nature become animated,
at day break, and succumb quietly
to the colors of night.

People scamper about. Families enjoy
the waning days of summer. Store
clerks eagerly assist customers
buying sea shells, T-shirts and other
gifts, which along with tans and
sunburns, will provide evidence
of vacationing, at an ocean-side resort.

Waitresses and waiters, serve platters
of appealing food, and quickly snatch
away empty plates from sated customers
There is hugging, kissing, hand-holding
everywhere.

Continued

All these observations of life cycling
widens the gulf between us, because
I want to dwell on a past lost, and a
future I can't have without your
presence. I know it is time to map
a new life, but I don't know if I can,
because you took all the rainbows
when you left.

*This is another poem written about my deceased spouse, Carl
Edward Young, Jr.*

VIRGINIA BEACH HANG-OUT

My family's favorite hang-out at
Virginia Beach used to be Seaside
Amusement Park. The building that
once housed a restaurant, games,
and children's rides, stands idle, in
pregnant silence, its doors tightly locked.

Nose pressed against the dirty
window pane, I search for a
familiar sign of life: but there
isn't any—even the spider who
built the large cobweb hanging in
the corner, no longer can be sighted.

Never again will mother, son, and
father waltz down the boardwalk to
buy a soft ice-cream cone with
chocolate coating—no more
chili dogs with mustard—or hot
buttered popcorn, will be purchased
after late night walks on the beach.

We will search for a new place to
seek food and entertainment,
but new-and-improved, won't
replace Seaside Amusement Park.

My family enjoyed many trips to Virginia Beach. As soon as we were settled in our motel, my son, Andrew (or Andy as most know him), had to visit Seaside Amusement Park. New places sprouted, but while nice to visit, we never became as socially or emotionally attached to the other places.

PROSE POEM FOR GRANDMOTHER

I search out Grandmother in the urine-soaked holding bin, called a nursing home, where she has existed these last years. She can't be found in bed today, screaming from pain, caused by those inoperable gallstones, so says her physician.

She is in the lounge, sitting in a row with other residents, all strapped into wheelchairs. All little carbon copies of each other: freshly scrubbed, and perfumed; those alert waiting eagerly for visitors on this fourth of July holiday. Some residents stare blindly at the television. Some snooze. Grandmother is napping. She makes little puffs with her lips as she takes runtish breaths. Her head droops so low it almost touches her withered breasts.

I lift the leg quilt that covers her legs. The lower portion of Grandmother's flowered dress has been scrunched into a roll; a sheet is stuffed between her legs. The sheet serves as a diaper so that Grandma won't urinate, or worse defecate, on her clothing. It's a good thing Grandmother's brain is muddled because she would violently protest this indignity.

I gently rub Grandmother's hands, tracing the snake-like, purple-black veins that course under her taunt, almost transparent skin. Since Grandmother does not hear well, I crunch my face to her ear, shake her gently, and ask, "Do you know who I am?" There is no sign of recognition.

Continued

I move close to her again, tell her, *It's your favorite granddaughter.* These are words she used to tell me, and while I think it quite likely she said the same thing to all her granddaughters, I still loved hearing them.

My words register. She leans toward me. Her weak cataract eyes bore intently into mine. I search for a tissue to whisk the mucous off her upper lip; she has a drippy nose. I reach for her hand, pull it toward my face, speak loudly and slowly, *Hello, Grandmother. I love you.*

Grandmother rubs my cheek with her hand. A big smile breaks through paper-thin lips.

Some images in "Prose Poem for Grandmother" were gleaned from observations of nursing home residents, and, consequently, all were not my Grandmother's experience.

The rubbing of my cheek is one of the favorite memories I retain of Grandmother America Lee (Powers) Fletcher.

THE ROAD WE MUST TRAVEL ALONE

In the nursing home
Grandma sits, strapped in
her nursing home chair:

humble, dependent, defeated.

Life seeps from her bones, inchmeal.
with ever-increasing finality, her
body decomposes.

I haven't discarded her.
But it's too late to take
her away from this place,
because death
is only a whisper away.

This poem was written for my grandmother, America Lee (Powers) Fletcher. Her daughter, Wanda Lee (Fletcher) Meade, was my mother. Grandmother Fletcher was one of the great role models in my life, and I loved her dearly. She was a woman who "thought outside of the box." She had little formal education, but I remember her as an astute, self-taught business woman who could "stretch a dollar for a mile." She was a woman devoted to her family. I don't think there was a selfish bone in her body.

REMEMBERING MAMA MARY

There must have been a time when Mama
didn't have white hair, although I see only
her beautiful pallid hair, twisted into a rigid
bun, from which nary a hair ever tried to
escape so that it could fly freely in the wind.
Those hairs all knew that bolting the confines
of her Chignon indeed would be futile. Instead,
each strand patiently waited to be freed from
imprisonment; all confident that Mama
eventually would eradicate hair pins that kept
the coil compactly attached to the nape of her
neck. After tendrils were loosened, silky
strands of hair danced in unison, as each
cascaded down her shoulders. Mama would
vigorously stroke her hair, with a favorite
stiff-bristled brush. Each stroke, creating static
electricity that caused the hairs to stand at
attention. After brushing concluded, the best
part of the day began. Mama would pull me
upon her lap, and devote a few previous
minutes to tell me how much I was loved.

*This poem was written in honor of Mary Elizabeth (Moore) Meade,
my paternal grandmother.*

ELEANOR LANNEAU (GILDERSLEEVE) YOUNG
(February 24, 1923 - October 14, 2009)

Eleanor died peacefully: a blessing,
surely; but those in her circle, still
fought her going, when at age 86,
she took flight to Heaven. Eleanor,
we remember: the young girl starting
to blossom, into womanhood—her
world cracked, and never fully
mended, when her parents, together,
died tragically; but Eleanor, with
willful mind, and strong hands, always
ferociously flung, discouraged tears,
to the wind. High school beauty, she
found Carl; they married, on the day
of Pearl Harbor. Eleanor, dressed
blissfully thereafter, in wifely colors;
set her sights, on birthing the future:
Son, Carl Jr., soon appeared; followed
by Mildred, Patricia, and George.
Eleanor cocooned, all family in love;
gently placed dreams, to be considered,
upon their faces; helped each discover,
the best path to follow; fed souls, with
loving words of inspiration, from food
harvested, in her tender heart. Eleanor
produced sunshine, by affectionately,
kneading roles: wife, mother, grandmother.

*Eleanor Young was my mother-in-law. She was dearly loved,
and I miss sharing my life with her.*

PROSE POEM FOR MOTHER (1)

It's a slow process getting Mother ready for the appointment with the geriatric psychiatrist. Long-term depression. Numerous strokes. Dementia. Open heart surgery. Chemical imbalances. Medications swallowed far too long that have caused an ulcerated stomach.

Mother hardly can lift her arms today. Getting her out of the tub is extremely difficult; but she never liked showers. I lather pleated skin with lotion. Remark that I don't like the looks of the inverted nipple and huge areola. Note that I must make an appointment for her to see a gynecologist. I hook Mother into her bra. Arrange sagging breasts in the cups to increase her comfort: chide myself, remembering that Mother likely doesn't know comfort anymore.

I stop my routine to let her use the bathroom. Check to see if she cleaned herself. Demeaning, but these days Mother's trips to the bathroom generally end in a mess. I still let her do things by herself when she can summon a splinter of her short-term memory. Maybe completing such tasks gives her a sense of normalcy. Perhaps I need the familiarity.

She smiles at me and speaks my name. I'm overjoyed that Mother temporarily has triumphed over the tenacious enemy stealing her personality. This will be the highlight of our day.

My mother, Wanda Lee (Fletcher) Meade, died in November 2003. She left a void that can't be filled. I miss her immensely.

A GIFT FOR MOTHER
A Poem for Wanda Lee (Fletcher) Meade

I seized a moonbeam
to provide light for your feisty
soul as it journeys into infinity.

I seized a moonbeam
to illuminate your path as you
waltz through those Pearly Gates.

I seized a moonbeam
because I remember how
you always loved to dance.

I observed my Mother "cutting the rug" a few times, but I did not learn until after her death that dancing was one of her favorite pastimes when she was a young woman. I love to dance, too, and I wish Mother and I could have shared this passion.

I know so little about Mom's life before she became a wife and mother, and I feel a great sense of loss that the person she was in the early years of her life always will be unknown to me. I often wonder about things such as her dreams, aspirations, fears, and disappointments.

HAIKU

The following poems, written in the Haiku format, are some of my favorites. I enjoy writing Haiku poetry because it is tremendously challenging to fit a few words into a coherent line.

The generally accepted format for Haiku is seventeen syllables—with five syllables in line one, seven in line two, and five in line three—although there are frequent deviations from this structure. In "The Haiku," Literary Cavalcade, author Suzi Mee states that, "Some poets consider the writing of Haiku to be a useful exercise, much the same as practicing the scales of a piano. But Haiku masters consider it the ultimate art form, involving observation, concentration, imagination, language, skill—and, most of all, surprise."

After initially reading Mee's statement, I wonder if perhaps I fulfill my life-long desire to learn to play piano by writing Haiku. I have to retract the previous statement in that I actually did learn to play a one-handed tune—Chop Sticks—on the piano which my Aunt Margaret (Meade) Wyatt taught me how to play. (She played the left-hand portion; I played the right-hand portion.) I don't recall the name of the song, but I remember a few lines of the song: "Take me in your arms and never let me go; whisper to me softly while the moon is low."

MY CAT SHADOW DANCER

Little furry face
my cat, Shadow Dancer
love unconditional.

Sleeping at my side
dreaming about birds
my cat smiles.

Sublime feeling
cat fur rubbing
against human skin.

Happily content
she melts upon my chest
offering licks.

HAIKU FUSION

In the inky night
deer seeking moisture gobble
leaves from the roses.

One yellow rose blooms
in spite of defoliation
by the thirsty deer.

Eyes shut tightly I
listen to leaves dingle as
they soar to the ground.

Apples rotting in
bowl: opportunity
missed again.

Chimes make known the
arrival of the wind:
leaves brace for a fight.

Brave grasshopper
clinging to the car windshield
hoping to survive.

Butterfly singing
happy songs of thankfulness
for summer blossoms.

BLISSFULNESS

The feel of cat fur
against human skin is
velvet blissfulness

HUMANIZED HAIKU (1)

Her needle snakes through
the white material: a
prick splashes on red.

BEACH HAIKU

Gulls adeptly soar
lifting my spirits as they
fly intemperate.

Waves lull me into
tranquility, quelling my
tempestuous soul.

Mollusks bequeath their
homes so I can blissfully
cull sea shells at dawn.

Published–The Piedmont Writer

FOUR SEASONS HAIKU

Spring Crocus court each
other in a melodious dance
of joyful rebirth

Bees gossip smugly
as they pollinate Lilies
in the summer sun

Autumn leaves bathe the
delighted forest in a
rainbow of color

Snow falls virginal
carapacing the earth
on breaths of calm silence.

Published–Branches in My Hand

NEW

To introduce this section, I'm going to record some thoughts about writing as a whole. One of the most rewarding and biggest assets to my writing life is my membership in the Blue Ridge Chapter, Virginia Writers Club. I have developed wonderful new friendships, and I have been stimulated by interaction with other writers (via meetings, workshops, guest appearances, and special and social events). The advice and excellent critiques of my work additionally has been immensely beneficial.

Another plus of my BRC membership is that I have been forced out of my comfort zone. I recently have reflected extensively about why I write, and what I want, or need, to achieve out of the process. I have been forced to reveal more of myself, because closing off the past, to a large degree, has hindered, or crippled, my writing in many aspects. All of the self-examination has allowed me to take new directions with my writing, including my experimenting with different genres and themes.

Slivers of my life experiences are illuminated in the poems included throughout my book. Some poems were difficult to compose and share, especially several included in this section. Yet, the process was rewarding in that I sometimes was able to grieve, heal, or let go of the past— all affirmation of the power of the written word.

THE HIGH PRICE

She intensely sweeps with a worn broom,
makes fierce attempts to destroy dust dancing
in the corners of her multi-purpose kitchen,
a domestic ritual repeated over and over,
because the kitchen is the place where she:

> Prepares meals
> Feeds her family
> Washes clothes
> Pays bills
> Helps children with homework.

She thrusts a mop into a pail of hot soap suds
and bleach water; jerks it out, expertly squeezes
water, stabs briskly at ugly stains left on the
worn linoleum by a variety of children's toys,
and years of shuffling feet encased in cheap shoes.
Stains refuse to budge. Her swiping never stops
because the floor is the place where her:

> New baby crawls
> Son and father wrestle before bed
> The new shelter puppy pees.

The chipped porcelain bathtub is vigorously
scoured with Ajax and sometimes ammonia,
but these stains have tenure, and will not budge.
Corner dust rebirths regularly; it keeps on twirling.

Continued

She can't erase the scarlet letter earned
long ago in a field of sun-kissed Daisies.
Her sin debased her reputation, sullied
the family name. Society deems it
necessary to persistently chastise.

Enveloped in night colors, she sits at the
kitchen table—her body as rigid as
the souls of those, who forced their own
transgressions into oblivion, as nonchalantly
as using White-Out, to erase charcoaled
words, from the newly-typed page.

Scandal-mongering never will end.
Eyes that talk with icy words won't die.
Nothing will scour away wrongdoing.
Sin can't be placed in a coffin and buried.

She momentarily regrets her first born
Was not aborted, feels remorse for
harboring this heinous thought, fears
the wrath of her vengeful God, the one
she has revered since childhood.

Emotionally malnourished, her eyes fixate
on the flowered plastic curtains, busily
marching docile shadows, along paint-starved
walls. She listens to her soul weep. Thinks
about the loaded gun, waiting in the hall closet.

*"The High Price" is dedicated to all women who have suffered
needlessly at the hands of those who hold power over their lives
for whatever reason.*

QUESTIONS

What is it about Southerners? Why do we suppress
and refuse to discuss the misfortunes, excruciating
experiences and past mistakes that bind as tightly to us as
the lining that ensconces our pulsating hearts?

Why don't we give voices to the secrets we unsuccessfully
strive to entomb, in order to deflect the stab of a
scandal-monger who has a chamber pot soul,
the one who is entertained by making others squirm?

Why do we banish excruciating happenstances into the
deepest fissures of our minds, thus allowing ill-fated
recollections and fear of unsheathing to gnaw at our
gut—like rats fighting for a piece of sloughed off cheese?

Why do self-important mortals derive such
Machiavellian pleasure from picking incessantly at the
imperfections and weaknesses they so much enjoy
identifying in others?

Where is the thrill in endlessly jabbing at a long-festered
wound? What happened to "Love thy neighbor as
thyself?"

To compassion?
To mercy?

"Questions" is a companion piece to "The High Price."
While I realize that emotional or physical abuse is not unique to
Southerners, I chose to focus this poem in the part of the world
that I know best.

A POEM FOR MY GRANDMOTHER: AMERICA LEE (POWERS) FLETCHER

Grandmother stopped living yesterday
after lying weeks

Knotted

in a fetal position.

She looks so beautiful
in her death pose.

Surrounded

by coronets of white satin
every strand of gray hair
groomed carefully into place

Round
Pearl earrings
Encircled

with gold, fill the

Holes

in her ear lobes.

Continued

A strand of perfectly shaped

Orbs

Of pearls repose upon her chest.

The ring she constantly twirled

Around

her finger because it was too large
shines brightly against the royal blue
dress with white

Ovals

the dress that will join her in eternity.

The family

Pirouettes

Grandmother's casket.

Some weep and embrace
while others carry on

Circuitous

conversations, debating
whether she should be buried
with her ring and her watch.

Continued

Their flat
Squared-off

words hang precariously in the
funeral-scented air.

They should know
nothing matters because
our circle has been broken.

Grandmother is gone
Her name was America.

I attempted in "Poem For My Grandmother" to show different types of "life circles" that are forever lost due to the death of an important family member such as a grandmother. The "circles" end in my poem when the "flat," "squared-off" words appear— just as our family circle irretrievably was broken when Grandmother Fletcher died.

Grandmother America (Powers) Fletcher was one of the most influential people in my life. Widowed at a young age with young children, she was forced into the role of family bread winner. She bravely tackled every hardship life presented, and she never relinquished her positive outlook on life.

TWO-SIDED BOOKS

Those glasses:
 Libby brand, the ones etched with
 silver boarders and leaves;

Those glasses:
 residing in my new China cabinet
 the cabinet purchased after my
 second marriage;

Those glasses:
 Mother obtained with S&H Green Stamps
 issued to entice customers to make
 purchases at our small-town grocery;

Those glasses:
 resulting from the proliferation
 of stamps I helped Mother paste
 into rectangular books as we worked
 late into the night, seated on
 unfeeling wooden chairs, our eyes
 taxed from working by dim light,
 cast by the lone sixty-watt bulb,
 dangling from the ceiling fixture,
 the globe cover, long ago broken.

Those stamps:
 affording us an opportunity, to be
 together, mother and daughter, making
 small talk as we labored—words I no
 longer can recall.

Those stamps:
>   helping me imprint memories,
>   never to be forgotten; recollections,
>   birthed in spite of the tedious process,
>   of filling books full of minute squares,
>   with green stamps, many tongue-licked,
>   to moisten foul-tasting glue.
>   engorged books exchanged by Mother
>   for gifts, needed or desired, like

Those glasses:
>   Mother gave me as a wedding present—
>   the ones used with my expensive China:
>   Royal Doulton, Coronet, cream-white in color.

Those glasses:
>   The set with the silver rims,
>   placed on the table on special
>   occasions only;

Those glasses:
>   that pleasantly link my past to the present:
>   a place now visited in memory only—
>   where Mom and I, again sit side by side
>   ssometimes lost in unfastened
>   thoughts, as we attentively paste
>   S&H Green Stamps into two-sided books.

My mother, Wanda Lee (Fletcher) Meade, collected S&H Green Stamps and I occasionally helped her paste the stamps into "little books full of minute squares." Mother did most of the pasting, though, and I frankly never enjoyed the tedious stamp-pasting job.

I did receive Libby water glasses as a wedding gift (along with other gifts purchased with S&H stamps that I no longer can recall). These glasses are a treasure to me. Some years ago I was thrilled to find Libby wine glasses in an antique shop that matched my set.

REMEMBRANCE ON HIS
SEVENTIETH BIRTHDAY
(A Poem for my spouse, Larry Lee Rubendall)

I remember how excited I became on
the first day of school: I put on a
newly-starched shirt and brand
new spit-polished shoes.

Filled with anticipation, I grabbed
my yet-to-be-used supplies:
pencils, paper, erasers, a ruler,
and best of all, another box of Crayola
Crayons, in all the latest colors, including
my favorite: Sun-kissed Yellow.

Each one stood tall, in its designated spot,
not a blemish to be found anywhere,
all wrapped snugly, in a strip of paper
that announced the name of each
sumptuous tint.

I carefully protected my prize
possession, since I soon would be
coloring—my youthful passion.

Crayons were put to other uses,
like drawing maps of the United
States—an assignment given by
my second grade teacher, Miss
Nance Broady, who insisted her
students memorize the state capitols.

Continued

School was lots of fun, but no
experience equaled day one,
when the school yard was
punctuated with scrubbed faces,
and fresh smells: clothes, shoes,
books, papers, and me—proudly
wearing a few splashes of Dad's
Old Spice Cologne (in spite of
the fact I got teased because I had a
different comprehension of *splashes*,
than did my classmates).

Nothing equaled my love of
Crayola Crayons: I could not
wait to pull them from the box,
to aid me in developing artistic
fingers.

*This poem highlights some of the fond memories my spouse has of
his early elementary school days—memories that are closely linked
with colors and smells of new things. It is marvelous that we
develop such savory and lasting memories about something as
simple as clothing worn and supplies carried on the first day of
school.*

SEARCHING FOR A CHRISTIAN

Sally goes to church every time the doors are open.
She always sits proudly in the front row pew,
dressed to the hilt in her bright red Pendleton suit.
A model Christian Sally always appears to be,
although she makes fun of Susie who is grossly
overweight, saying that Susie should keep her mouth
zipped, so that she won't eat quite so much.
>   Is this a Christian?

Joe knows one day in Heaven he will be, for he has
been saved, and diligently he obeys the Written Word,
except that Joe embezzles from his company,
to pay for a beach condo at Nags Head, and doing
this deed doesn't bother his conscience at all.
>   Is this a Christian?

Rosie is puffed up and arrogant, since
God called her to minister to His Brethren.
She knows the Bible from cover to cover;
speaks eloquently, too. But Rosie chastises her
flock, saying they won't get to Heaven until they
Conform, and learn to emulate her.
>   Is this a Christian?

Sam and Ruth have always been devout Christians.
Raised five children in the church, also, but their
son, Peter, they knew him not, after learning he
was gay and had AIDS. Peter died alone, racked
by disease and rejection.
>   Is this a Christian?

Continued

The Pope is a religious man in God's image indeed.
They think him so god-like he can do no wrong.
Much admired and respected is the Pope, even though
He continues to enforce the church's control over
women, by saying NO to birth control and abortion.
And as a the Ruler Supreme, he denies woman any
role of importance, in all the extraordinarily rich
Catholic churches . . . while he offers blessings, seldom
ever any money . . . to help the plight of the poor.
Is this a Christian?

Tina quit going to church long ago; gave it up
after some fellow Christians criticized her to
the junior high students, Tina taught in Sunday
school, just because Tina didn't attend a Pizza
party, missed due to exhaustion from being up all
night, walking the floor with her baby son.
Is this a Christian?

Ben is a charismatic television minister.
People are so touched by his tears and prayers,
that rich and poor, give him all their hard-earned,
or inherited dollars, which Ben uses to frequent
prostitutes, and to install solid gold fixtures, in his
two-million dollar home, the one sitting on twelve
acres.
Is this a Christian?

Continued

Mark is a superb Catholic priest. His life
has been a perfect example, of devotion
to God and His Spiritual Kingdom, but
Mark sexually molests young choir boys,
Whose parents have entrusted their
children into his care.
        Is this a Christian?

There also is Jane, whose ovarian cancer keeps her
from attending a House of Worship. But Jane has
Faith. She has accepted Christ as her Savior. Jane
looks forward to being out of pain soon, when she
joins God, and He makes her whole once again.
        Is this a Christian?

Jerry doesn't go to church, but he was saved and
baptized. A physician in a university hospital
emergency room, Jerry spends his free time
working for Hospice and the local Free Clinic.
He gives free physicals at inner-city schools.
        Is this a Christian?

John is a Deacon in the Church of God.
John's job is guarding prisoners in the state
Penitentiary. He adheres faithfully to the Ten
Commandments—except one—John believes
it is necessary for him to turn on the switch to
the electric chair, to kill those criminals who
exist in cages.John thinks these men are too
horrendous to inhabit the earth.
        Is this a Christian?

Continued

Jack and Ruby are foster parents.
They clothe their multi-racial family, at Sears.
This couple doesn't have a car, or money for
the family to take a bus, so they don't go to
church often. But Jack and Ruby still try to
worship with their children, when possible.
        Is this a Christian?

*I wrote "Searching For A Christian" as part of a term paper about
AIDS and the book,* The Band Played On, *while a student at
Piedmont Virginia Community College (Charlottesville, Virginia).
The course was entitled "Contemporary Religious Thought." The
class was an enriching one that made me, and I believe the entire
class, think about the true meaning of being a Christian.*

*   The class professor was a youth minister who most often
was employed on a college campus. I was very touched when this
professor wrote me a letter after she had accepted a new job in
New York. She told me she kept my poem posted on the bulletin
board located outside her office. I often wonder how many times
my poem has been read. I hope the reading has generated a great
deal of conversation, and debate, as took place in our classroom.*

WHIMSICAL, LIGHT VERSE
OR JUST PLAIN NONSENSE

Writing poems that fall into the "whimsical, light verse or just plain nonsense category" always is fun. While I certainly did not have a good time when ill with Swine Flu, writing the poem made me chuckle. There is nothing that can be said about "Bad Poems About Periods" except it is totally awful. The other poems all have a special place in my heart because of evoked memories.

SWINE FLU

It's appropriate to call you, Swine Flu,
because H1N1 is to milk toast
for the Router-Rooter
of my gastrointestinal tract.
You who visited,
uninvited and unwanted,
Thanksgiving 2009.
Relentless foe: You forced me
to hug the toilet, all those hours,
while I erupted, on opposite ends,
like a Yellow-Stone Geyser,
refusing containment.
You burped, hiccupped,
and gassed me,
through five days of torture.
My strength so completely plucked,
I could not remove the lid
from a tube of Neosporin,
to place soothing salve
on my inflamed a-hole.
With tornado speed,
you ravaged my body,
filled every orifice with
noxious fumes and sick poison.
Just as I thought dying preferable,
you seized with laughter,
made your exit,
moved silently, to another victim.

DESIGNER THWARTED

Paper dolls used to mesmerize me
when I was a little girl.
I spent hours creating colorful and
trendy outfits for my store-bought
slivers of dolls: I fashioned
      fancy evening dresses
      suits and skirts
      eye-catching hats
      bathing suits
      and coats.
Exacting tabs, meticulously scissored
held my masterpieces snugly in place
upon the bodies of my fine, flat ladies
who along with their outfits galore
were stored neatly in shoe boxes.
I know:
      Von Furstenberg, Claiborne,
      Prada or Gucci
would have hired me in a
New York minute, had Mother not
incinerated my masterpieces, in our
humungous old coal stove.

BAD POEM ABOUT PERIODS

I declare empathically that I need periods galore
to stop my words from proliferating as I pen
all those less than wonderful verses // while
evermore hoping that I soon will be published . . .
Just when I start to run amuck // getting much
frustrated // a period comes calling to tell me
all I have to do is cut some words full of vowels
and eliminate those over-used clichés most foul . . .
I then will be able to hone my creative-writing skills
so that scripting verse soon will bring the applause . . .
But right now lines I etch onto paper are quite stilted . . .
For the life of me I can't conjure up images to be quilted
to lines that previously were quite painstakingly created . . .
So I find it necessary to bring my poem to a screeching
halt // by stopping all movement with a period at the end . . .
I mop at perspiration // not so daintily / / say to hell with it all
and watch another period leak swiftly from my pen and fall
right into place at the end of a distressfully mediocre stanza . . .
Well // there is no doubt // I'll keep on collecting periods
by the ton . . . Thinking // a famous writer // someday I still
will become . . . This is why I love periods // every darn one . . .

*This poem was submitted to the 2009 "Bad Poetry Contest" sponsored
by the Poetry Society of Virginia. The request was for submission of
one "very bad" or even "horrible" poem. I am surmising my poem
wasn't horrible enough since it didn't place.*

SPIN

Can't recall much about
the early years of my life.
Do clearly remember, playing
Spin-the-Bottle, at my
sixteenth birthday party.
Friends of both sexes, my sister
and I (she really too young to
have participated), sat circled
in the grass, under the waning sun,
all impatiently waiting our turn,
to whirl the Coca Cola bottle.
My spin landed at DW's feet.
He electrified my lips,
when we kissed, in my parents.
dilapidated smokehouse: the place
where I fell, hopelessly in love, for
the first time, for about fifteen minutes.

When I was sixteen, we had to make our own entertainment at birthday parties, and Spin-the-Bottle always was a popular "game" to play. Common food and beverage items served at a birthday party would have included Kool-Aid; RC Cola; homemade Lemonade; potato chips and dip; finger sandwiches (maybe even peanut butter and jelly, and tuna fish); cake and ice-cream. There were no theme parties hosted at a local restaurants, no gourmet foods served, no expensive presents given, but it was my sixteenth birthday, and having a party that included my best friends and the neighborhood gang was terrific.

HILTON HEAD FAMILY VACATION (2005)

Three sisters, a brother, and spouses all
arrived on September 10 . . . vehicles stuffed
with possessions . . . little room left for asses . . .
but it didn't matter since we were all together . . .

Larry said Lauvonda mothered too much . . .
but it comes to her natural, she says . . . since she
began babysitting while still a youngster herself . . .
but it didn't matter since we were all together . . .

Our time-share condo could have been better . . .
Palmetto bugs ran unbridled in mattresses dreadful . . .
We got enough backaches to last a century . . .
but it didn't matter since we were all together . . .

Debbie and Cliff insisted on sleeping every night . . .
on the awful sofa bed that afforded no privacy . . .
Their generosity allowed us to be selfish . . .
but it didn't matter since we were all together . . .

Kim, our banana-pudding-maker extraordinaire . . .
watched all the football games . . . and finished her
shopping before we had time to get started . . .
but it didn't matter since we were all together . . .

Our hearts were saddened by the continued . . .
catastrophic condition of Robert's crushed feet . . .
Sorry also we were that Lauvonda lost her diamond
ring . . . but it didn't matter since we were all together . . .

Continued

Nurse Kim took care of feet wrappings . . .
with the greatest of ease . . . and Lauvonda gave
pretty good massages with her untrained fingers . . .
which made us all happy while we were together . . .

Cliff surprised us all by bicycling . . .
and agreeing to go parasailing . . .
We think he had more fun than anyone . . .
which made us all happy while we were together . . .

Larry entertained all of us with his dancing and wit . . .
and he won hands down for doing the most cycling . . .
We were overjoyed to get Robert on a bike, too . . .
which made us all happy while we were together . . .

Bud kept us organized . . . that's the engineer in him . . .
Our computer whiz . . . he also kept busy . . .
burning photo and music disks . . . for us . . .
which made us all happy while we were together . . .

Debbie colored her hair . . . painted the gal's nails . . .
We hope sometime she will undertake training . . .
to become a professional . . . but . . . we like freebies . . .
which made us all happy while we were together . . .

Christine, our professional house cleaner, couldn't . . .
stop looking for dust balls even on vacation . . .
She helped us make great decisions about purchases . . .
which made us all happy while we were together . . .

Everyone enjoyed . . . great food and drink . . .
especially the oysters, shrimp, and Margaritas . . .
Found in the restaurants . . . dotting the island . . .
which made us all happy while we were together . . .

Continued

Our one made-at-home-breakfast . . . was surely a treat . . .
gravy, biscuits, eggs, sausage, and bacon inclusive . . .
We gobbled down every calorie with great delight . . .
which made us all happy while we were together . . .

On a pleasant Trolley ride in Savannah . . . we learned . . .
the city's history . . . were visually stimulated . . .
Our free meal at the Conch House was awesome . . .
which made us all happy while we were together . . .

The hours spent listening to a salesman natter . . . about
a "time-share purchase" . . . wasn't too hard to endure . . .
since the free gifts . . . including a cruise . . . were terrific . . .
which made us all happy while we were together . . .

We felt visited by Dad . . . while studying Robert's face . . .
and mother was present in many conversations . . .
It was nice to have them with us in spirit . . .
which made us all happy while we were together . . .

Lauvonda and Larry, Christine and Bud . . . took pleasure
in our Friday trip to Buford and Huntington State Park . . .
where one of us took a time out to piss in the ocean . . .
which made us all happy while we were together . . .

As we left the island on that last day . . .
We felt renewed love for each other . . .
Our thoughts were about . . . the great
experiences shared . . . Hearts all sang
with joy . . . because we were so grateful . . .
we had this time together . . .

MY FAVORITE

Old Blue Water Bed Sheet
Proudly still granting pleasure
although discolored with age
much frayed, and increasingly
plagued by unwelcomed cavities.

Old Blue Water Bed Sheet:
Not mine originally, inherited
via marriage: Worthless as a drilled
nickel to most, but still my favorite,
for lying contently in the sand, while
I'm soaking up rays, waiting patiently,
for Basel Cell Carcinomas.

Old Blue Water Bed Sheet:
You always are my first choice to use
when I play Kissing Monster in the
backyard with the grandchildren, or
take them for picnics at Sherando Lake.

Old Blue Water Bed Sheet:
You are the keeper of all my secrets,
the best, the worst: Like the time
my spouse and I used you as a bed,
in the secluded spot, we found in North
Garden, that night after the office party
ended at Sven's: the inky evening that

Continued

we cautiously stepped over knee-high
weeds, to fling you on top of assorted
clusters of field greens, in the hope that
we would be protected from contact
with any Poison Ivy, that might wish
to kiss skin unaware, while we gleefully
copulated, as night began to leisurely
dissipate into morning: an act we
committed, in spite of our fear of being
caught, and charged with indecent exposure,
or with committing a lewd and lascivious act
in public:

Old Blue Water Bed Sheet:
No tight-collared policeman stepped
out of the darkness, to shine a bright light
into our grinning faces, that not-to-be-forgotten
summer night, but it would have behooved us
to have paid more attention, to where we
stepped and placed our body parts, since it
didn't take long for the dreaded blisters
to appear, in tender places, that made it
exceedingly difficult to scratch demurely,
while we attempted to escape, inquisitive
public eyes:

Thanks for your steely silence
Old Blue Water Bed Sheet.

RECIPES

The recipes in this section hold special memories because they have been prepared and shared with love over the years by women in my family, many who have been mentioned in this book. A few are my own reformulated concoctions whereby I've attempted to recreate family recipes that were never written down. I share them here as a legacy for future generations of our family.

I begin this section with my poem, "Cooking Up Love" which was written in a creative writing class when I was a student at Piedmont Virginia Community College (Charlottesville, Virginia). We students were given a list of words, about fifteen as I recall, with instructions to write a poem or short prose piece using the words. I never helped my grandmothers cook, but I really adore this created memory. This poem speaks to the importance of bonding between family members which so often happens in the kitchen while cooking together. It also illustrates how the ingredient of "love" can build bridges and heal broken hearts.

Finally, I end this section and this book with a special poem and recipes for my grandchildren.

COOKING UP LOVE

Grandma prepares Thanksgiving dinner.
Stuffed turkey roasts in the oven.
A multitude of luscious odors mingle in
the air: Butter, onion, cornbread, celery,
sage. Fresh cooked green beans and beets
add more pithy fragrance to the air. My
stomach growls with anticipation.

I'm Grandma's official helper: washing
dishes, cleaning vegetables, dicing,
fetching, setting the table. My biggest
holiday job is assembling the sweet
potato casserole. Grandma adores the way
I add extra brown sugar, cinnamon, and plump
marshmallows. An assortment of cakes and pies
already are lined up in a row on the kitchen
cabinet. Grandma baked yesterday. There will
be plenty for everyone.

I get Grandma hugs, frequently. She keeps
mentioning I'm doing a fine job. Often tells
me how much she loves me. Her words
warm my heart today, just like the old gas
stove has amply heated the kitchen.

Working with Grandma momentarily makes me
forget the recent death of my little brother, who
no longer will join us for Thanksgiving dinner.

WHITE LILY "LIGHT" BISCUITS
From the Kitchen of Lauvonda Lynn (Meade) Young

2 cups White Lily Self-Rising Flour; 1/4 cup shortening; 2/3 to 3/4 cups milk, or more (regular or buttermilk).

Preheat oven to 500 degrees. Measure flour into bowl (spoon into measuring cup and level off). Cut in shortening until mixture resembles coarse crumbs. Blend in just enough milk with fork until dough leaves sides of bowl. (Note: I generally add a dab more milk, because insufficient moisture makes the biscuit too dry.) Knead dough gently on a lightly floured surface, 2 or 3 strokes. Roll dough about 1/2 inch thick. Cut biscuits with floured biscuit cutter. Bake on ungreased baking sheet, 1 inch apart for crusty biscuits, almost touching for soft sides; bake for 8-10 minutes (adjust baking time to individual ovens). Serve immediately. Makes twelve 2-inch biscuits.

Additional notes: (1) For tender biscuits always handle dough gently and use as little extra flour for kneading and rolling as is possible. Kneading or handling the biscuit dough too much produces "tough" biscuits. (2) Brushing biscuits just out of the oven with some melted butter is a nice touch. (3) White Lily flour makes the best biscuits! (I used to make White Lily biscuits using regular flour, but the ones made with White Lily Self-Rising flour are just as good.) (4) I often add cheese, sometimes herbs and other seasonings, and make drop biscuits. Kneading is not required for drop biscuits. (5) Some cinnamon, nutmeg, nuts, and sugar can be added to this recipe to make a sweet biscuit for breakfast.

MAMA'S BUTTERMILK BISCUITS
From the Kitchen of Mary (Moore) Meade

2 cups self-rising flour; 1/4 cup Crisco shortening; buttermilk.

Place flour and Crisco in a large bowl. Blend in Crisco with hands until very lumpy. Make indention or well in center of flour mixture. Begin by adding 1/2 cup buttermilk. Add additional buttermilk as needed to reach lump consistency. Pour onto a floured dough board; knead and roll out with pin to 3/4 inch thickness. Cut with a biscuit cutter or glass top dipped in flour. Place in a pan with 2 tablespoons of shortening heated in a 400 degree oven, dipping both sides of the biscuit in the melted shortening. Bake until brown. Brush tops of biscuits with butter while hot.

My Grandmother Meade (known as Mama) was famous for her breakfast of Chocolate Syrup, biscuits, and home-churned butter. When I used to eat breakfast at her house, she let me have my own (full bottle) of RC Cola. There always were several meats to chose from, as well, usually in combinations of two: bacon, sausage, ham, country ham, and probably pork chops because my southern family often ate pork chops for breakfast.

ELEANOR'S REFRIGERATOR ROLLS
From the Kitchen of
Eleanor Lanneau (Gildersleeve) Young

Sponge: 1 cup mashed potatoes (lukewarm); 1 cup milk, scalded and cooled; 1/2 cup sugar; 1 package yeast, dissolved in 1/4 cup warm water.
  Beat in 1/2 cups flour into the above mixture. Mix well. Cover and let rise 1 hour.
  Dough: Add to the above: 2 eggs well beaten; 2/3 cups melted shortening; 2 teaspoons salt; flour sufficient to make a soft dough.
  Grease top of dough; cover with Reynolds Wrap and store in the refrigerator overnight. Next day, shape into rolls. Brush lightly with butter when placed in a baking pan. Let rise until double in bulk or about 2 hours. Bake in a 350 or 400 degree oven for approximately 20 minutes, or until brown. Makes about 30 rolls.

My mother-in-law, Eleanor Young, a marvelous cook, never used a recipe to make her rolls. She once told me she started cooking at age 12. Her rolls were "World Famous" in our family. Her cooking expertise was widely known, and she loved preparing meals for family and friends. For many years, she was manager of an elementary school cafeteria; it was the most popular place in town to eat lunch. Mom Eleanor and her husband, Carl Edward Young, Sr., made bread and sold it to a convenience store for a number of years after they retired (he from the post office, she from food service management). She made the bread; Carl helped, but his major jobs were to slice and package the finished product. Eleanor made bread and mailed it to her children and grandchildren. I always was happy to see her package arrive.

ELECTRIC FRY PAN MEATLOAF
From the Kitchen of Lauvonda Lynn (Meade) Young

1-1/2 pounds ground beef; 3/4 cup old fashioned oatmeal, uncooked; 1-1/2 teaspoons salt; 1/4 teaspoon pepper;
1/4 cup chopped onion (not instant); 1 8-ounce can tomato sauce;
1 egg, slightly beaten

Combine all ingredients thoroughly. Pack firmly into a 9x4-inch loaf pan. In a preheated electric skillet at 225 degrees, melt 1 tablespoon butter. Remove meat loaf from pan, place in skillet and bake, covered with vent closed, for 30 minutes. Carefully turn meat loaf to second side. Continue to bake for an additional 15 to 20 minutes. Let stand 5 minutes before slicing. Makes 8 servings.

Note: I most often add additional spices such as sage and dry mustard. (Your own favorites can be added.)

I mentioned earlier the meatloaf my mother, Wanda Lee (Fletcher) Meade, used to prepare. She "passed down" very few recipes. I believe she mostly cooked from memory or past observation. I found this recipe and modified it to be very similar to how Mother made it.

FRIED POTATOES
From the Kitchen of Lauvonda Lynn (Meade) Young

Peel and cut potatoes into chunks (fairly small chunks); prepare as many potatoes as you need for your meal. Dice some onion, to preference (I mostly use white onion in my cooking); sometimes I add a little diced green pepper, but this ingredient is not essential. Add (to preference) salt and pepper (add a few flakes of hot red pepper if you like a little heat); a dash of dry mustard is a good addition; (other herbs can be added; sometimes I use dill weed or rosemary—use fresh rosemary sparingly, as it is a strong herb); celery seed or garlic also can be added.

An iron skillet works best to prepare this recipe. Place oil of preference in the skillet and heat (I use Canola oil most of the time these days, with a few pieces of butter added to enhance the flavor.) "In the old day," I used bacon grease—honest truth—it wonderfully flavors foods such as Fried Potatoes, and it was a staple when I was growing up.

I used to think that Aunt Marty and I prepared Fried Potatoes on her miniature stove in her play house, but perhaps not since she tells me she had the "Easy Bake Oven," which I don't think had a burner. Maybe my memory is of the many times that my sister, Linda Christine Meade, and I used to cook in one of the outbuildings on our farm. We built a fireplace of cinderblocks and made a pit in the middle. We cooked potato soup, corn on the cob, and other foods from ingredients we raided from the garden. I don't know how we kept from setting the building on fire, or how we concealed such dangerous mischief from our mother.

SWEET POTATO CASSEROLE
From the Kitchen of Lauvonda Lynn (Meade) Young

6-7 sweet potatoes, medium sized, peeled, cubed; 1 can sweetened condensed milk (only half of the can will be used); nutmeg (to taste; freshly grated is best); a dash of salt; butter (a few teaspoons, to taste); 1/2 cup (or more) chopped Pecans (or other nut of choice); 1 bag mini-marshmallows.

Boil potatoes until cooked (test by poking with a fork). Drain water from potatoes. (Note: Canned sweet potatoes can be substituted, but fresh cooked always is better.) Beat potatoes with a mixer until they are free from lumps. Add salt, butter, nutmeg. Mix in half of the can of sweetened condensed milk. Whip thoroughly. Pour mixture into a baking dish. Sprinkle on Pecans. Top with marshmallows.

Bake for 15-20 minutes, or until marshmallows are lightly browned, in a 300 degree oven

This recipe does not contain any brown sugar, but I make a version of Sweet Potato Casserole sometimes which calls for the use of brown sugar. I think brown sugar enhances the flavor of sweet potatoes. I sometimes add a different topping and omit the marshmallows.

A DIFFERENT TOPPING
1/2 whole-wheat or white flour; 1/3 cup packed brown sugar; 4 teaspoons frozen orange juice concentrate; 1 tablespoon canola oil; 1 tablespoon butter, melted; 1/2 cup chopped Pecans. Mix all except Pecans in a small bowl, until crumbly. Add Pecans. Spread over the top of the casserole.

BEETS IN ORANGE SAUCE
From the Kitchen of Lauvonda Lynn (Meade) Young

8 whole fresh beets; 1/4 cup white sugar; 2 teaspoons cornstarch; dash black pepper; dash salt; 1 cup orange juice; 1 medium navel orange, halved and sliced (optional); 1/2 teaspoon orange peel.

Place beets in a large saucepan; cover with water; bring to a boil; reduce heat; cover and cook for 25-30 minutes, or until tender. Drain and cool slightly. Peel and slice; place in a serving bowl and keep warm.

In a small saucepan, combine the sugar, cornstarch, pepper, and salt; stir in orange juice until smooth; bring to a boil; cook and stir for 2 minutes, or until thickened; remove from heat; stir in orange slices if desired and peel; pour over beats; Yield: 8 servings.

Note: A 15 ounce can of sliced beets may be substituted for the fresh beets. Drain the canned beets and omit the first step of the recipe.

MOM'S FRIED GREEN TOMATOES
From the Kitchen of Wanda Lee (Fletcher) Meade

Wash and slice green tomatoes (as many as you need). Salt, pepper, and dust a little sugar on each side of the tomato (sugar is my Mom's addition). Let them sit for a couple of minutes while the coating supplies are being assembled. Put some white flour and corn meal (the corn meal is my addition) in a bowl (you may need to replenish several times depending on the number of tomato slices to be fried). Put some eggs in another bowl (I generally start with four; sometimes I have to add more). Add some salt, sugar, and pepper to the eggs. Some milk or water can be added to the egg mixture to thin it, if desired). Note: Salt, sugar, and pepper measurements can be done to taste; omit pepper if desired.

Using oil of preference (Canola, Olive, bacon grease, butter, or a combination thereof); I generally use Canola with a few tablespoons of butter to add flavor), fry tomato slices until brown on each side, turning as necessary, and adding more oil as needed. I believe an electric fry pan does the nicest Fried Green Tomatoes, but an iron skillet also can be used.

I prefer ketchup on my Fried Green Tomatoes. Heinz is my favorite store-bought brand, but I use other ketchups like the recipes on the next page.

SPICY KETCHUP
From the Kitchen of Lauvonda Lynn (Meade) Young

2 tablespoons onion, or to taste preference (I like lots of onion in my recipes, and I prefer white onion.); 1 large clove of garlic, chopped (or 2 small cloves of garlic, or use garlic powder if you don't have fresh garlic on hand.); 2 teaspoons Canola oil; 2 tablespoons brown sugar; 2 teaspoons cumin seeds; 1 inch piece cinnamon stick; 3 cayenne peppers, minced I don't use this many cayenne peppers because I dislike too much heat; ground cayenne can be used; the heat can be controlled better). 1 chipotle pepper in adobo sauce; 6 ounce can tomato paste; 2 tablespoons cider vinegar; 1 cup water.

In a 2 quart saucepan over medium heat, combine the garlic and oil. Sauté for about 5 minutes, or until just beginning to color. Add the brown sugar, cumin seeds and cinnamon stick. Cook for another 2 minutes. Add both peppers, the tomato paste and vinegar. Simmer for 10 minutes, stirring frequently. Add the water and return to a simmer.

Pour through a mesh strainer, or blend in blender, to remove any solids. Set aside to cool before using.

QUICK & TASTY HOMEMADE KETCHUP
6 ounce can tomato paste; 1/4 to 1/3 cup tap water (depends on consistency desired); 2 tablespoons vinegar; 1/4 teaspoon dry mustard; 1/4 teaspoon cinnamon; 1/4 teaspoon salt; 1 pinch cloves; 1 pinch allspice; 1 pinch cayenne pepper; 1/4 cup brown sugar.

In a medium bowl, combine all ingredients. Whick, blending well. Scrape the mixture into a small pint jar or container that can be sealed. Chill overnight to blend flavors.

FOR MY GRANDCHILDREN

My blood does not
course through the veins
of the two that call me
Grandma.
I climbed into their
family tree, via a second
marriage to their *Grandpa.*
It really is quite easy to see,
that the composition of blood,
isn't all that critical, because all
grandchildren really need, is a
grandparent who loves them,
unconditionally. They especially
like a big playmate, who lets them
make all the rules; and my beloved
granddaughter is quite adept at
establishing new rules on the spot.
She always appears elated when
I attend her numerous tea parties,
where she serves up tepid water,
instead of real tea. Sometimes
our teas are accompanied by
whipped cream and chocolate
covered raisins, or a smattering of
Cottage Cheese, or a sand box cake.

Continued

Right now grandson, nine months
of age, is crawling and has just
learned to stand. Adored by his
Grandma, Daniel always has a
sweet smile for everyone. He loves
to be held, while his holder walks;
and he gets very vocal, when the big
feet, become inactive, for any reason.
Daniel and his big sister have a mutual
admiration society. I feel blessed every
time I hear one of my grandchildren,
call me *Grammy*. I certainly am having too
much fun, to give genes a moment's thought.
In the final analysis, I don't need to see,
my features mirrored, in my grandchildren's
faces. It makes me happier to think,
Grandma Lynn is imprinting in their hearts.

*I have a standing joke with my grandchildren. Whenever I
see them, I say, "How are my two favorite grandchildren?" or
"How is my favorite granddaughter (or grandson)?" I only
have two grandchildren, and when I make this statement,
my granddaughter always responds, "Grandma, you only have
two grandchildren." I reply, "I know, and this is why you are
my favorites."*

*Laura and Daniel, the children of David and Karen
Rubendall, are the newest loves of my life. It is divine to watch
them experience life without encumbrances and restraints—
everything is new and interesting to them.*

LEMONADE

5-6 lemons; 3 quarts of water, or to taste depending on tardiness of lemons; 3/4 cup Maple syrup (or to taste). Squeeze lemons. Add water and maple syrup. Refrigerate to cool. Note: Thin slices of lemons added to the lemonade will enhance the flavor.

CHOCOLATE CAKE

MIX TOGETHER: 1 (8 ounce) package cream cheese, at room temperature; 2 (1 pound) boxes powdered sugar, sifted; 1 teaspoon vanilla; 1 stick butter, at room temperature, 5 squares unsweetened chocolate, melted; 1/2 cup milk, at room temperature. DIVIDE this mixture in half. One half will be used to ice the cake.

MIX TOGETHER: 1/2 of the above mixture; 2-1/2 cups flour; 1/3 cup butter; 4 eggs; 1 1/2 cups milk; dash of salt; 1 teaspoon baking powder; 1 teaspoon baking soda.

PLACE cake mixture in 2 round 9-inch baking pans, or in an appropriate size square baking pan, greased. BAKE at 350 degrees for 30-40 minutes. COOL and ice with remaining cream cheese mixture.

Note: I add nuts (usually pecans) either to the cake batter or the icing.

CHOCOLATE SYRUP
From the Kitchen of Mary (Moore) Meade

2 cups sugar; 1/2 cup cocoa powder; 3/4 cup water

Mix all ingredients together in a pot and boil until it thickens, stirring frequently. If it boils over, add a teaspoon of butter to the mixture. Serve over hot, buttered biscuits. Leftovers can be stored in the refrigerator. Very good, also, poured over ice cream, cake, or fruit.

GRAMMY'S PUMPKIN BREAD FOR DANIEL
Family Recipe—updated by Lauvonda Lynn (Meade) Young

Mix together: 1 cup oil; 3 cups white sugar; 4 eggs, slightly beaten; 1 can pumpkin or 2 cups fresh pumpkin. (Recipe says if canned pumpkin used, add 1/2 cup water and beat, BUT I don't add the water as I think the bread is more moist without the water added.)

Sift together: 3 1/2 cups flour (all purpose); 1/2 teaspoon baking powder; 2 teaspoon soda; 1 teaspoon cloves; 1 teaspoon allspice; 1 teaspoon cinnamon; 1 teaspoon salt; some grated nutmeg to taste (my addition).

Mix wet with dry ingredients. May fold in 1/2 to 1 cup nuts, of choice or 1/2 to 1 cup candied cherries; I don't add either one when making bread for Daniel.

Pour batter into greased, floured pans. Bake at 350 degrees for about an hour. (I use throw-away baking pans when baking gift items.)

LAURA'S PLAY DOUGH

This is not a recipe created by Laura. I'm just including it because her name is in the title. This play dough is not edible. It is great for a rainy day project or a last minute birthday gift that a child will love.

1 cup white flour; 1/2 cup salt; 2 tablespoons cream of tartar; 1 table-spoon oil; 1 cup water; food coloring.

Mix flour, salt, cream of tartar and oil in a saucepan. Add water and mix well. Cook over medium heat, stirring constantly for 3 minutes. Dough will become difficult to stir and form a clump. Knead for 5 minutes. Add drops of food coloring during kneading process.

This keeps a long time if stored in a covered plastic container.

LAURA'S SAND BOX CAKE
(Recited to Grandma Lynn by Laura, around age 4)

5 cups sugar
5 cups flour
5 cups milk

Mix well. Place in baking pan. Bake 5 hours.

I suppose Laura was fixated on the number 5 on this particular day! (Note: Not for consumption, of course!)

ABOUT THE AUTHOR

Lauvonda Lynn (Meade) Young
currently resides in
Palmyra, Virginia,
with her husband
Larry Lee Rubendall;
her cat, Shadow Dancer,
and a humungous collection of
books (especially poetry, cookbooks,
and an eclectic selection of fiction
and non-fiction, many autographed)
that fill all the nooks
and crannies of her home.
She has adopted her spouse's
goal to live long enough
to read all of her books (including
cookbooks) so she voraciously
continues adding to her collections.

FEB   2012

Breinigsville, PA USA
14 March 2011
257638BV00001B/6/P